The Whitetail Fieldbook
The Visual Guide to Deer

Michael H. Francis

NATURE

Available from Nova Vista Publishing
Business Books
Win-Win Selling
Vendre gagnant-gagnant (French edition of Win-Win Selling)
Versatile Selling
S'adapter à mieux vendre (French edition of Versatile Selling)
Social Styles Handbook
I Just Love My Job!
Taking Charge of Your Career Workbook
Grown-Up Leadership
Grown-Up Leadership Workbook
Time Out for Leaders
Time Out for Salespeople
Leading Innovation
Service Excellence @ Novell
What Makes Silicon Valley Tick?
Nature Books
Return of the Wolf
The Whitetail Fieldbook
Music Books
Let Your Music Soar

How to order: single copies may be ordered online at www.novavistapub.com and at book stores. In North America, you may phone 503-548-7597. Elsewhere, please dial +32 476 360 989.

ISBN 90-77256-12-1

D/2006/9797/2

Printed in Singapore

20 19 18 17 16 15 14 13 12 11 10 9 8 7 6 5 4 3

Editorial development: Molly Grooms, Steve Grooms and John Kelley
Cover and text design: Astrid De Deyne

CONTENTS

FOREWORD

Sometimes you create your own luck. By getting out in the woods, especially during the early morning and late afternoon, you greatly increase your chances of seeing wildlife.

And sometimes, you are rewarded with a once-in-a-lifetime sighting, like the one I had recently in the North Dakota Badlands. I was looking for deer, but few were visible that year. A disease (EHD, or epizootic hemorrhagic disease) had spread upstream along the Little Missouri river and killed off many of the whitetails living nearby… no wonder I had been seeing so many eagles feeding along the river!

Not willing to give up, I kept searching for deer. Finally, one evening, just minutes before sunset, I spotted a coyote attacking a young buck who was standing in a small stream.

I was prepared with high-speed film and the water also reflected the fading light, so I was able to photograph the life and death struggle taking place before my eyes. Both the coyote and deer were exhausted when the sun went down and I lost sight of them.

The next morning I went back to find just a skull, a few bones and some hair – the buck had lost the fight. I'm sure he was weakened by disease, because otherwise a single coyote would not have been successful in bringing him down.

I have had many other memorable experiences with deer through the years as I have photographed them, seeking them from Quebec Province to Florida, across the entire continent to the Pacific, and far north into the Rockies and western Canadian provinces. I invite you to share the discoveries of my journeys into deer country and to deepen your understanding of this remarkable creature.

Michael H. Francis

PART 1
THE YEAR OF THE DEER

SPRING

Let's start our fieldbook with the birth of white-tail fawns in the spring of the year. They appeal to our romantic notions of deer, but in reality they live a precarious existence and have only about one chance in two of growing up.

Most mothers give birth to twin fawns, which helps to ensure that some survive to perpetuate the species. Unfortunately, not all newborns make it through the early stages of life, as weather and predators take their toll. ▼

Newborn fawns spend their first week or so hidden from the world. Their spotted coats serve as camouflage. When approached, they reduce their breathing and heart rates until danger has passed. An undisturbed fawn will rest with its head up, ready to bolt or to assume a hiding posture as soon as danger threatens. ▲

Established females have traditional fawning areas which they aggressively protect from other deer. These older does are the most successful mothers, as they have learned from previous years how best to rear a fawn through the seasons. ▲

The doe nurses and grooms the youngster several times per day. While nursing, she licks the fawn's genital area to stimulate it to urinate and defecate. ▶

As the fawns grow older they become more adventuresome. Twins often investigate their surroundings together. At this age they can outrun many predators, as they now have an understanding of their home range and its many hiding spots. ▲

One look at those big eyes and baby face, and you can see why generations of nature lovers have been enchanted by little Bambis. Fawns this young rarely spend much time up and about, even though they are capable of traveling a considerable distance. It is much too dangerous for them to move around, with predators such as bears, coyotes, wolves, eagles, wild cats, and domestic dogs out looking for a tasty fawn morsel. ▶

Fawns may be abandoned by their mothers for a number of reasons. Without the care of the doe, the fawns are subject to predation and starvation. Fawns are picked up by humans because they may seem abandoned. It is best to leave them where you find them, as the mother is usually nearby, nervously awaiting your departure. ▲

As the fawn grows older it starts to nibble at plants, but will continue to nurse for a few more months. ▶

Alert to danger, this spotted youngster is racing to the woods with tail held high to alert others. ▲

Just like mother. Fawns are great mimics of adults. An experienced mother is the best teacher. ◀

Not only is spring the birthing season for white-tailed deer, but it is also the time of antler growth for males (and rarely, for females). Antlers drop off each year and grow anew each spring. ▲

Fawns born to well-nourished does have the best chance for survival. This fawn appears to be thriving on its mother's milk and nutritious forage. ▼

Only members of the deer family grow antlers. Other species grow horns. Healthy, mature bucks typically start antler growth and new hair growth earlier in the spring than younger or unhealthy males. ▼

A fawn needs to stay close to its mother and follow all the cues she gives. ▲

 SUMMER

Summer is the easiest part of the year for whitetails, as they eat, loaf around, put on fat and generally enjoy life.

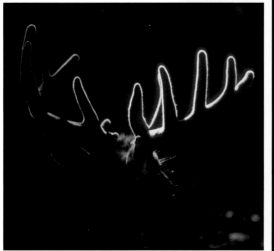

Antlers are among the fastest-growing formations in the animal kingdom, growing at the rate of a quarter of an inch (6 mm) per day. They grow most rapidly during the summer months, with most of the development happening during June and July. During this time, antlers are quite soft and can be easily damaged. ▲

A magnificent mature buck in the early morning. Deer tend to feed most heavily during the early morning hours of darkness. He is probably looking for a place to bed near the crest of a hill where he can monitor potential danger throughout the rest of the day. ▲

These are this young buck's first real set of antlers. He is now around 12 months old. ▶

Deer antlers have long fascinated humans. They grow as living tissue and are actually bone. A growing antler is supplied with blood through the many blood vessels in its protective velvet covering and through the core. If an antler is damaged while in velvet, it may grow misshapen. ▲

In his prime, this large, mature buck displays non-typical antlers. A master forager, he has found nutrition enough to maintain a large, healthy body as well as grow a large set of antlers. Producing antlers takes a huge toll on a buck's body, equivalent to the drain on females who are nursing. The payoff comes during the rut, because does choose conspicuously successful bucks when pairing up for mating. ▶

Odocoileus virginianus is the Latin name for white-tail deer. The species gets its name from the large tail, which is white on the underside and ranges from brown to black on top. When a deer is alarmed, it raises its tail and flares its hair. This white flare signals danger to deer in the area, putting them on alert. ▲

In early summer, yearling bucks disperse to join bachelor groups of older bucks. Here a young buck is being welcomed into the fraternity by a large mature buck. ▲

During the summer months, living in their bachelor groups, bucks are buddies. They pal around together, enjoying each other's company. That changes once their antlers harden and they become rivals for female companionship. These bucks are growing their gray fall coats over their red-brown summer ones, and their antlers are now fully grown. ▶

In many areas, whitetails have overcome their fear of man and have moved into back yards to take advantage of plantings and gardens. In some yards they are welcome, while in others they are considered pests. ▼

Grooming is part of the daily ritual for healthy whitetails. Since whitetails are social animals, mutual grooming also serves to strengthen bonds between individuals. ▶

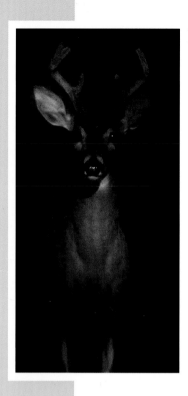

A younger buck in velvet antlers. In terms of mortality, yearlings are the least vulnerable and the oldest deer the most. Few deer reach old age, especially in hunted populations. ◀

Deer are quick to find and colonize fertile areas such as this recent fire burn in Montana. ▼

It is thought that antlers help dissipate heat during the warmth of summer. ▲

Always an opportunist, this buck is harvesting fallen apples. He seems to have one caught in his teeth. ▶

Deer utilize a variety of habitats. This doe is searching for lush vegetation along a pond shoreline in Maine. ▶

Whitetails are drawn to water. Here a doe finds a small pool of rainwater in the depression of a boulder in the midst of the forest. ▼

Whitetails are opportunistic and adaptable in their feeding habits. Surprisingly, some have even been observed scavenging on fish carcasses. But they prefer the most tender and nutritious parts of plants, the newest shoots and leaves. As ruminants, they quickly ingest their foods without having to chew it thoroughly. When bedded safely, they then take the time to regurgitate the cud and re-chew it into smaller mouthfuls. ◀

A large, mature buck with fully grown antlers. It's just a matter of time before the velvet starts to crack and the process of cleaning the hardened antlers will begin. The longer hairs of his fall coat are already visible. ▶

Summer is a time of plenty. Except for hot weather and biting insects, this is an easy time for the deer. Now is the time for a mature buck such as this one to put on weight so he can get through the upcoming rut and the cold winter months. ◀

By late June or early July, velvet growth on the antlers is well on its way. The size and shape of a buck's rack are determined by a combination of genetics and nutrition. ▶

Deer are active after sunset. Like other nocturnal animals, they have a membrane in the back of their eyes that reflects light back through the receptor layer of the retina. It's called a *tapetum lucidum*, and it enhances their night vision. It also produces the eye shine shown here with the camera flash. ◀

It is important for does to feed well during the warm summer months. Not only are they still nursing fawns, but they are also growing a new coat, both of which need considerable energy reserves. By building a healthy body, they also prepare for the twin challenges of surviving winter and producing from one to three strong fawns in the spring. ▲

In order for bucks to grow large bodies and antlers, they need to have considerable amounts of nutritious forage available through the spring and summer months. ▶

FALL

Fall is my favorite time of year. Cool mornings, warm days, leaves changing colors and, best of all, the biting bugs are gone. Deer are at their absolute peak, with prime coats and hard antlers.

A prime non-typical buck with asymmetric antlers surveys his territory. His enlarged neck shows he is rutting. ▲

During the fall, when a buck's antlers are fully grown, the velvet starts to die as blood flow stops. The dead and dying material starts to shrivel, crack and peel off. This must feel irritating, because the buck rubs and thrashes branches and vegetation to remove the velvet. ▼

Rubbing to remove the velvet also gives the buck a good idea of the size and shape of the antlers he has grown this year. Some bucks bleed profusely, while others show little blood. The amount of bleeding in conjunction with the various plant juices determines the coloration of the buck's rack. Bucks sometimes stop rubbing and eat the strands of velvet that hang from the rack and vegetation. Now they are ready for some sparring. ▲

As summer turns to fall, gradually the spotted coat of the fawn turns to one that is colored like its mother's. Soon it will grow long, hollow guard hairs, which help insulate by trapping air. Since they are waterproof, they also help keep the fawn's shorter, insulating undercoat dry. ▲

Even though fawns have coats that are similar to the adults', they still keep a baby face through the winter months. They are much more independent from their mothers now, although the bond between them remains strong. ▶

A young buck with first-year antlers. He is learning to stay away from the larger bucks during this season, even though he is curious about the rut. He actually is mature enough to breed, but probably won't if larger bucks are in the area. ◀

It's a bit unusual to see two large fawns still nursing during the fall mating season. Usually by now the doe has long since weaned her youngsters. The cost of lactation is high for a female, and at this time of year she has to make sure her body is in good shape for the approaching winter challenges. ▶

The bond between a mother and her doe fawn may last through their lifetimes. This female has done a good job keeping her twins alive and prospering since their birth earlier in the spring. The young buck's "button" antlers show he's getting a rich diet. Most young bucks do not grow their first set of antlers until the following spring. ▼

Whitetail twins are often the best of friends. Females may indeed stay together for the rest of their lives in the same maternal clan.

After the first freeze of the autumn, many plants that were toxic earlier become palatable. This is a pleasant time of year for the doe, as she can now concentrate on putting on weight to survive the coming winter months. By now most females have weaned their fawns. ▶

Portrait of an alert mature doe in her fall coat. Few things in her territory escape her acute sense of hearing, smell, and eyesight. ▲

A mature buck takes a break and grooms himself. ▶

Deer pellets on the forest floor. During the summer months, the droppings are much softer and less defined than in the fall and winter. ▲

The antlers are cleaned and the leaves are changing color. This signals the start of autumn and rut-related activities. In most of North America, the rut spans a couple of months, starting in October and ending in December, but it may extend into February or March in the southern US. ▶

In farm country, deer can cause extensive damage to cash crops. This deer is obviously well fed on corn. Cropland in North America supports high densities of deer. ▶

A buck searching for acorns after the fall rut. This is a critical time for bucks who have been active during the rut. They have been so busy chasing and defending does that their feeding has been curtailed. Now they must gain back weight before the snow flies. Large antlers such as his may be an advantage in winning does, but may also be a mixed blessing, as dominant males often die at a younger age as a result of stress and injuries that come from fighting. ▼

WINTER

Winter is a dramatic period when both males and females are tested and must literally fight for their survival.

Deer are quick to utilize foods sources even if they are not meant for them! In the winter, haystacks in the open are fair game for the deer. Unfortunately, after deer have defecated and urinated on the stacks, the hay becomes unpalatable to cattle. ▶

Rutting bucks enter winter at a great disadvantage. They may have lost as much as 25 percent of their body weight in the rut. Their fat supplies may be exhausted just when they need them the most. This leaves them susceptible to predators as well as to starvation. ◀

A young "spike" bucks feeds beneath Devils' Tower in Wyoming. The habitat here supports both whitetails and mule deer. ▼

Winter poses different challenges, depending on the habitat where the deer live. This Montana buck will see snow come and go as warm winds from California melt the snow from time to time throughout the winter. ▲

Disputes between does over food are often settled with a boxing match, both females flailing with front hooves while rearing up on their hind legs. ▲

Deer grazing on agricultural land in Wyoming. Whitetails gravitate toward irrigated fields and other places that support crops. ◀

An observer can make an educated guess about the sex of the animal which made the track, but the only way to be certain is to see the animal make the track!

The sign of a good mother: both her fawns are fat and sleek. She obviously knows where to find the best forage in her territory. She also knows the best escape routes to elude predators. ▶

In order for a doe to survive the winter months, she must be in good physical condition. Unlike bucks, who use up their fat reserves during the rut, the females feed continuously throughout the autumn months. ▼

Deer in the Northeast and Midwest often herd together in winter "yards." The terrain between resting and feeding areas becomes crisscrossed with deer trails. As snow deepens, almost all travel is confined to these deer highways. ▶

A young alert doe. Winter in Wyoming can be a mixed blessing. Snow is usually not as deep here as in the Midwest, but blizzards and wet, deep snow from spring snow storms can be deadly. ▶

Deep snow makes it difficult for deer to travel within their winter territory. It is also hard to access food sources. In snow this deep, it will be difficult for this individual to survive until spring. ▼

Hungry deer may resort to eating lichen and tree bark in heavy-snow years. In some years in the Great Lakes states, the die-off of starving deer can be staggering. In some regions they will migrate to areas where their winter survival chances are enhanced. ▼

The amount of body fat that does and fawns accumulate prior to winter can determine whether they survive the winter. ▲

The doe-fawn bond remains strong during the winter. The doe is the only real protection the youngster has from usurping deer who may wish to push the fawn from a food source. She also knows the trails to and from feeding areas and the important migration routes. Without a protective mother, it is very difficult for a fawn to survive. ◄

This fawn's long guard hairs are doing their job, protecting his underlying insulating hairs. Even in frigid weather, the fawn will stay comfortable. ►

Cold and deep snow are obstacles for all deer, more so for fawns. This Wisconsin youngster must fight to see next spring and warmer weather. Death among whitetails is a normal occurrence during winter, and fawns usually represent the bulk of winter deer losses. ◄

Healthy bucks are capable of withstanding severe weather and food deprivation during the normally frigid months of January and February. But when the snow starts early and ends late, it can be devastating to fat-depleted bucks. ▼

During the winter months bucks often leave the rest of the herd in order to find adequate food. This buck has already dropped his antlers. ▲

PART 2

WAYS OF WHITETAILS

HABITATS AND VARIATIONS

Whitetails are incredibly adaptable when it comes to habitat, and they are found in virtually every corner of North America. Some individuals may look quite unlike the others.

White-tailed deer are found throughout North America in various habitats. The deer thrive on the abundant nutrition of agricultural crops such as corn. Here in a cornfield, deer find not only food but a great hiding place as well. Deer can do substantial damage to farmers' crops. ▲

Deer are quick to colonize fire burn areas for the rich vegetation which flourishes for years afterward. ▶

Whitetails range widely over much of North America. The largest inhabit the northern United States and Canada. These deer stand about 40 inches (1 m) at the shoulder and weigh up to 400 pounds (180 kg). The Badlands of North Dakota offer good habitat along waterways. ◀

For some folks from the Northeast and Midwest, who are accustomed to seeing only glimpses of deer through deep woods, it can be a shock to see the same deer out in the open in places like Montana. ▲

Many deer call the swamps, palmetto, and Spanish moss of the South home. These deer are smaller in stature than their northern cousins. ▶

Whitetails in Texas have learned to live with extremes in heat. Although for the most part Texas deer are smaller than those in the north, many bucks do support large antlers for the size of their bodies. ▼

Deer throughout America have learned to live with humans, in some cases becoming a nuisance. With no natural predators, the population often increases to the point where car and deer collisions are a problem. ▲

The deer living on islands off the east coast of North America are much smaller than their mainland counterparts. The very smallest of these is the endangered Key Deer in Florida, with a typical large male weighing only 50 pounds (22 kg), about as much as a small Labrador retriever, and standing only 28 inches (71 cm) tall. ▲

Deer of the northern deciduous forest tend to be among the largest of North American deer. They generally grow the largest antlers. Their bodies have become larger to help conserve body heat during the frigid winter months. ▲

Whitetails coexist with a number of wildlife species, including pronghorn antelope on the grasslands of the west. ▶

A white-colored whitetail. They are often confused with an albino deer, but notice that the eyes are dark-colored, not pink like the eyes of an albino. This is just a genetic variant of the common whitetail coloration. ▲

Another colorful variant of the whitetail is the uncommon piebald deer. This female lives in a Florida swamp. ▲

White-tail deer and their close relatives, the mule deer of the west, are capable of interbreeding. Here a white-tail doe is checking out a mule deer buck in an aspen forest of Alberta, Canada. ◄

An albino fawn with its normal-colored mother. Albinos lack color pigment in their skin, hair and eyes. Notice that the eyes and muzzle are pink. Albinos are very sensitive to strong sunlight and often die at an early age. ▶

In some areas whitetails share their habitat with their larger cousin the elk. Because elk are larger, they have an edge in the competition for scarce food resources. ▼

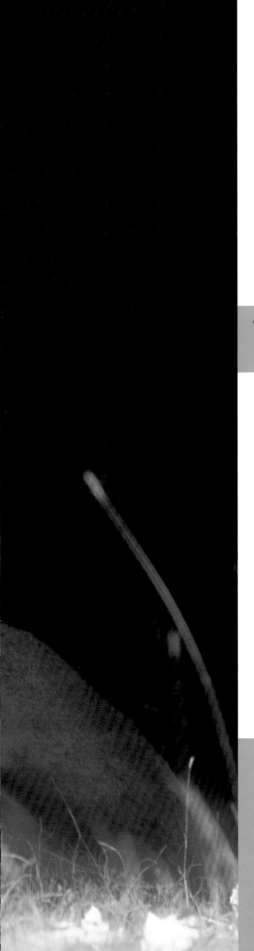

THE RUT

During the rut, males become magnificent in their quest for dominance and a chance to breed.

The courtship ritual involves the bucks chasing the does. The doe may keep the buck on the run for a day or two until she is ready to breed. She only allows the male to come near when she is fully receptive. ▲

For bucks in hunted populations, the rut is the most dangerous time of year. Why? High testosterone levels make bucks chase does all around the countryside, paying more attention to the does than to their own safety. This can lead them into open terrain where they are highly visible. ▶

During the rut, females release small amounts of urine to communicate their reproductive status to bucks. ▲

A lip-curl or flehmen. To test the readiness of a female to breed, the male licks the fresh urine which the doe has left on the ground. He draws chemicals from the urine to an organ on the roof of his mouth. From this he can determine whether the female is ready to breed. ▼

The tending bond. When a buck has found a doe in estrus, the pair forms a bond and they separate themselves from other deer. The buck remains close by, patiently waiting for a chance to copulate. He will also stand guard, chasing off rivals. ▲

If she is ready, a doe will often stand for closer inspection by the buck. If he smells that she is ready to breed, the buck will attempt to mount the doe. ◄

A curious young buck is chased off by the mature "tending" male. ▲

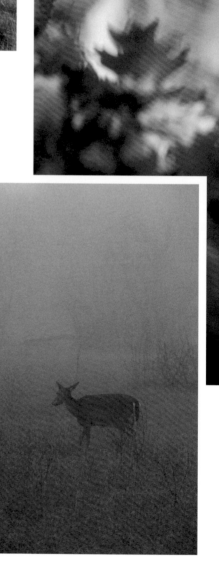

A mature buck does the "grunt-snort-wheeze." This threatening sound is performed by agitated bucks and can be made while they curl their lips. This buck was in a fight just moments before and has lost sight of the doe. ▲

Throughout the rut, bucks continue to approach and test the urine of does. Often they make a quick charge to startle females into urinating. ◄

Two Texas bucks sparring. Sparring is not fighting. Sparring takes place both before and after the rut. It allows bucks to test each other without fear of injury, as this sport is highly ritualized. It can best be described as a pushing and shoving match, similar to arm wrestling in humans. It is a way for bucks to learn where they belong in the social hierarchy. Often larger bucks tolerate challenges from smaller bucks during these tests of strength. ▲

It's easy to see that this buck is not happy: his body language displays clues of aggression and dominance. His ears are laid back along his neck, his eyes are staring, and his hair is standing on end, making his body look bigger. Often the nostrils are also flared. He is threatening aggression. A smaller buck will back off with a submissive gesture, but a buck of equal size may accept the challenge and a dominance fight may follow. ▶

A scrape, often beneath a scent-marked branch, gives a buck another means to signpost his presence in the area. The buck paws away leaves in about a three-foot square (one square meter) area, and then urinates on the bare soil while rubbing and urinating on the tarsal glands on his rear legs. This behavior is known as rub-urination. It is thought that both bucks and does that pass by can identify the male who created the scrape. ◀

Here a curious young buck is smelling the urine on the tarsal glands of an older buck in a swamp setting in Florida. ▲

Scent-marking branches is an important part of whitetail deer communication. The buck mouths the branch or rubs it with his forehead and pre-orbital glands, leaving a sign that he is in the area. Bucks may even stand on their hind legs to mark a branch. ◄

Both sexes will urinate on their rear hocks. During the rut some dominant bucks will urinate exclusively in the rub-urination position, staining their back legs. ▲

A buck investigates a scrape. ▲

A rubbed tree: a sure sign that a buck has been in the area. ◄

A buck working a rub will remove the bark and then scent-mark the lighter-colored wood with his forehead gland. Older bucks tend to make rubs on larger trees. These rubs serve as signposts and that are visited by both males and females. ▲

With no suitable tree to make a rub signpost, this buck uses the next best thing: a cypress knee in a Florida swamp. ▲

It's not just big mature bucks that make rubs. Here a young "spike" buck is making his own rub. ▼

All-out dominance fights are rare and usually do not last long. Unlike sparring, which is a friendly encounter amongst friends, a fight may go to the death. Injuries happen, antlers may be broken, or fighters may get gored. Fights typically occur between evenly matched combatants. ▲

Bucks can be quite seriously wounded during the rut. This young buck was gored by a larger buck, and his wounds are serious. As a result of his wounds, he dropped his antlers. ▲

Two evenly matched bucks in a dominance display walk. Both are displaying antlers, body size and attitude to the other. This may or may not end in a fight, as one may back down and run off, leaving the doe to the victor. ▶

On occasion, one of the combatants kills the other. A buck who is wounded may be repeatedly gored by other rival bucks while he is down or incapacitated. ▲

Injuries do happen during fights. This buck took an antler tine in the eye. ◀

A rutting buck uses his nose day and night in tracking down does. ▶

The rut is stressful for mature bucks, and by its end, they are exhausted. They now need rest and good nourishment to gain back lost weight and to heal their many injuries from fighting. ▶

The skull of a large, mature buck who died just as the rutting season was starting. This buck might have been gored in a fight, killed by a poacher, or disease may have caught up with him. ▼

A copulating pair in the open grasslands of Montana. During the mating season, normally secretive mature bucks show themselves in the open countryside. ▲

With the rigors of the rut behind them, bucks resume friendships. Here two groom each other in their bachelor group. ▶

Rut-weary bucks need to rest and restore their bodies quickly if they are to be ready for the stresses of cold weather, snow and reduced forage. This panting buck has been chasing a doe and jostling for a favored position with other males. Fall snowstorms in the northerly habitats add to the challenges that bucks face. ▶

Deer are fine swimmers and often cross large bodies of water. Here a buck crosses a stream during the rut. ▼

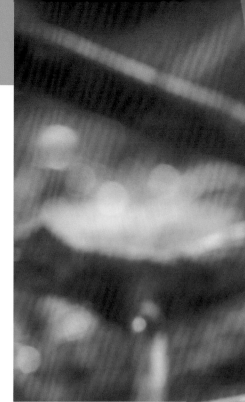

Bucks resume life in bachelor groups for the rest of the year after the rut. Friendly sparring sessions are common. ▼

Bucks are sometimes permanently wounded during fights. This buck lost sight in his eye a year earlier but has managed to survive the rigors of another rutting season. ▲

BEHAVIOR

You can observe complex patterns of behavior in the field as you spot whitetails going about their daily lives.

Typical whitetail feeding consists of finding the food, eating it rapidly, and consuming the food in the comfort of a safe spot. Only when they are bedded in this safe place do deer regurgitate the cud and chew it into smaller pieces. Because deer do not have upper incisors, they have to tear or pull on food sources rather than clipping it. ▶

Mutual grooming starts early in life and continues to be important throughout a deer's life. Grooming serves to reinforce the bonds between mothers and young, and between friends, whether male or female. One deer will remove unwanted ticks that the other cannot remove on its own. ◀

For both males and females grooming is an integral part of each day. ▼

For a large part of the year, deer are really quite lazy. Except for feeding periods, they spend most of their time lying around. ▼

Whitetail deer are natural athletes – they have to be to escape their many predators. Does leap eight-foot (2.5 m) fences with little effort. One deer researcher measured a buck's broad jump at 29 feet (9 m) going downhill. ▲

Rearing up on his hind legs and threatening a front kick, this young buck shows his displeasure at a fellow fawn. The young learn quickly – this signal is exactly what an antlerless adult would do. ▼

The sense of smell is the most important of the deer's senses. Deer constantly test the air for the scent of danger. Their sense of smell also helps deer to find and select foods. ▲

A buck breaks through the ice on a cool fall morning to get his drink. ▶

CHALLENGES

Whitetails face many challenges to their survival. They must cope with predators, disease, weather and accidents.

Bobcats prey on whitetails. Although the cats are small, they are fully capable of bringing down full-grown deer. Nocturnal hunters, once bobcats make a kill they remain in the area for several days, feeding heavily on the carcass. ▶

Wolves are major predators of deer in some parts of the country, especially the northern US states and in Canada. In winter the deep snow makes their job easier as the snow hampers the ability of the deer to escape. ◀

Black bears are not major predators of adult deer but they do seek out fawns in the spring. Carcasses from winter-kill deer are important sources of protein for bears when they first come out of hibernation. The protein that this carcass gives the bear should get him by until the spring green-up starts. ◀

Wolverines are the largest members of the weasel family. Although capable of taking prey, their keen noses also help in finding carcasses. In this case, a deer has washed up on the rocks and these wolverines are taking advantage of the opportunity. ▲

Many bird species will scavenge a carcass when the opportunity presents itself. Here an immature Harris Hawk is feeding on a deer carcass in Texas. ▶

A deer caught up in a fence is doomed to a long, agonizing death. A healthy deer should be able to leap a four- or five-foot (1.2 or 1.5 m) fence with no problem, but accidents do happen. ◀

While coyotes are fully capable of killing adult whitetails, the majority of their deer meals are fawns or carrion. This North Dakota coyote is attacking a young buck that is ill, most likely from a virus known as EHD (epizootic hemorrhagic disease). ▼

Although one parasite, the meningeal worm, is often carried by white-tail deer, it does them no harm. But it can be fatal to many other hoofed mammals, including moose. The worm infects the brain, eventually causing death. As deer density increases, the moose population will decrease. ▲

The white-tail deer is one of the favorite game species in North America. ▶

Deer die from many causes: injuries, old age, disease, accidents, predation, and starvation. It's not uncommon after a long hard winter to find many carcasses in areas where deer have wintered. It's just difficult to figure out what they died from. ▶

A man-made fatality. Motor vehicles kill more deer than hunters do. Here a rare endangered Florida Key Deer has been hit and killed on a road. ▶

Like humans, deer also can have a number of medical problems. This doe appears to have infected, enlarged lower jaws. ▲

Nothing is wasted in nature. Already the flies, maggots and carrion-eaters have cleaned up the remains of this Texas buck. The skull and antlers are all that is left. ▲

Magpies have discovered this buck which was hit by a vehicle. Many animals depend on carcasses to survive the winter. ▼

Introduced exotics (such as this Fallow Deer) can be problems for native wildlife such as white-tail deer. Exotics may carry diseases for which whitetails have no immunity. The introduced species may also be able to compete more successfully for valuable natural resources.

ANTLERS

People are fascinated by antlers and have been for ages. They are an amazing form of life in their own right.

Bucks go through stages with antler growth as they age and mature. If lucky, a fawn will develop "buttons" during its first summer. Typically young bucks will grow their first set of antlers when they are a year old. These antlers are usually in spike or fork form. In the following years the rack will continue to grow wider, with longer tines and more mass.

Most bucks don't make it to old age. As we see with this individual, their antlers gradually grow in smaller and smaller each year after their prime. This regressing buck carries small, poorly-shaped antlers and is going blind. ▶

Antlers can come in many shapes and sizes. Some bucks have extremely impressive headgear with numerous tines. ◀

This Texas buck has an unusual double main beam on one side of his rack. Each buck tends to grow a distinctive pattern of antler, and although his antlers might be bigger each year, they follow the same identifiable blueprint. ▲

Often when a buck has suffered a wound, the injury shows up the next year on the antler of his opposite side. This mature buck has seen his share of dominance fights. His brow tine is almost as big and massive as the main beam, an unusual formation. ▶

A pair of drop tines comes off this Texas buck's antlers. He is in poor condition coming out of the rut. ▲

Here a buck is growing a drop tine off of one side of the antler. ▶

This buck also probably suffered some damage to his antler while it was in velvet. ▶

Injuries do occur while antlers are in velvet. Severe damage can make them misshapen. This young South Dakota buck injured his antler earlier and sports one that is downward-hanging with a club end, while his other is typical. He will probably always grow an oddly-shaped antler on this side. ▼

A dropped antler that rodents have gnawed on. Rodents love to chew on antlers. They are great sources of calcium for many small animals. ▲

A young buck has recently dropped his antler. ◀

Some populations of bucks seem to grow very high, narrow racks. ▶

ABOUT THE AUTHOR

Michael H. Francis, *trained as a biologist, is an internationally renowned wildlife photographer based in Montana, USA. His photography has been internationally recognized for its beautiful and informative imagery. He has thirty single-photographer books to his credit, including* Yellowstone Memories: 30 Years of Photographs and Stories. *He is the main photographer for* Return of the Wolf, *written by Steve Grooms.*

Mike maintains a stock file of over 500,000 images. His work has been published by the National Geographic Society, The Audubon Society, The National Wildlife Federation; and Field & Stream, Outdoor Life *and* Sports Afield *magazines, among many others. Mike's photos for this book come from his archive of more than 25,000 deer images.*

Mike is an active member of the North American Nature Photography Association and served as its president in 2003. He regularly leads wildlife photography trips throughout North American. He lives in Billings, Montana with his wife, two daughters, and 15 turtles and tortoises.